MORE
GHOSTS AND HAUNTINGS
FROM THE
EAST RIDING

Researched by

Peter H. Robinson and Paul Hesp

With a Foreword by

Rev. Tom Willis

HUTTON PRESS

1988

Published by the Hutton Press Ltd.
130 Canada Drive, Cherry Burton, Beverley
East Yorkshire HU17 7SB

Printed and Bound by
Clifford Ward & Co. (Bridlington) Ltd.
55 West Street, Bridlington, East Yorkshire
YO15 3DZ

ISBN 0 907033 72 5

CONTENTS
The Second Collection

INTRODUCTION

When our first collection of ghost stories arrived in the shops, I breathed a sigh of relief. Our 'ghostly friends' and their hauntings were now respectfully recorded on paper; no more would I walk home glancing over my shoulder at that sound behind, or shiver as I passed a haunted property. Sleep, I could in peace now and without the light on; yes it's true, throughout my research I had many 'night terrors'. You see it's that vivid imagination of mine. I "see" practically everything I write or read, so I'm sure you will appreciate my welcome completion of the book.

But little did I realise the subject would be so popular, and with all age groups, selling out of the first printing in only ten weeks. Repeatedly readers of the book asked for more stories, as did our friends at Hutton Press.

So with a degree of reluctance, it was back to more ghosts and hauntings. Thankfully, we had a good few stories left over from the first collection, as well as a few new ones to research.

This time the stories come as an interesting assortment of hauntings along with some tales of the unexplained, including two murder mysteries. Repeatedly we questioned whether this material would be sufficient or interesting enough to make a second book. After lengthy deliberations we decided that 'yes' the contents would make a worthy sequel. We hope you think so too; but sadly our collection again is not complete for there were two more stories to add, one from what was once a cafe in Beverley Saturday Market Place, but try as we may, our source remained silent. The other from a large property in Hengate and although told episodically, I felt I wasn't really to know the facts behind the haunting.

There again, it's not impossible that one day if this collection is reprinted, we may just be able to sneak them in.

On now from my ramblings to acknowledging the team that have helped to make this book possible....

It was without question that Paul Hesp would join me again on the second collection of 'Ghosts', and with a repeat performance of enthusiasm he has shared, with my thanks, both the compilation and writing of this sequel.

5

A big thank you to Anita Wain, who again with great patience and care not only deciphered, but typed our original scribblings, and believe me that's what they literally were!

Our illustrators were so pleased at seeing their work published in the first Ghost collection that they waited eagerly in the wings to perform again, and so we present our 'regulars', firstly Steve Oldfield who has superbly portrayed many of the haunted properties, and as before our artists have been allowed licence to interpret the stories to the best of their imaginative abilities. They are Christine Cobham, Paul Wilson and Neil Andy Brown, who produced the excellent illustration for our front cover.

Newcomers to our arts team are Christine Townend, and Darren Limbert. Thanks to them all and we are sure you will agree their work is admirable and very worthy of inclusion.

Special thanks to our friends at Hutton Press, Charles and Dae Brook, whose help and encouragement has enabled this second collection to reach your bookshelf and thank you, our readers, for joining us and our 'ghostly friends' again.

Peter Harvatt Robinson
September 1988

FOREWORD

Every year in this country many thousands of normal, sane, healthy people see ghosts. Surveys have shown that one in ten people see at least one ghost during their lifetime, and one third of all such apparitions are witnessed by several people together.

To see a ghost, therefore, is not by any means a sign of a nervous, deranged or over-imaginative mind, but only a normal human experience.

Ghosts are a very real but mysterious part of our universe. Eye witness accounts present us with a wide variety of experiences. But no-one has been able to produce a comprehensive theory which explains them all.

The difficulty is that ghosts seem to be partly physical, partly mental and partly spiritual in their make up. They have a physical aspect in that they can be seen, felt and heard. They can be photographed and be seen reflected in a mirror.

Yet some apparitions appear to have no life of their own. They seem to be only an image of the past - a kind of video of someone's memory, of an incident which may have happened even hundreds of years previously. Sometimes they are simply images of objects which have never had life.

Other ghosts however do seem to have life and intelligence within them. They seem to want to communicate a message and have the characteristics of the traditional restless spirit.

The existence of ghosts cannot be explained at an entirely physical level. There seems also to be a strange spiritual distortion and disturbance connected with them. Happily the prayers and ministry of the Church can bring healing and peace to such hauntings.

Share now through the following pages of this book, more hauntings as experienced and told by the people of Yorkshire's East Riding.

Reverend Tom Willis
Bridlington
July 1988

ACKNOWLEDGEMENTS

Once again our acknowledgement list has not been easy to compile, respecting the wishes of those who were prepared to share their haunting experiences with us, but wished to remain anonymous. So as before and as requested in some stories we have changed the names, while in others, at the owner's request, properties are only identified by their being in a certain lane, street or road; and in total anonymity we have our section at the end of secret hauntings where the conditions of publication were not just a change of name, but that no indication of the geographical position be revealed. In every case we have respected their wishes, but still thank them all for allowing access not just to their stories, but sharing what is in many cases a very personal experience.

Our thanks to all the people listed below who had no reservations about their names being acknowledged. We sincerely thank them for making our second collection possible:

Paul Bird, Adrian Moore, Shirley Bagshaw, Paul Brook, Phil and Sheila Harrison, Kathie Spencer, Tom Barnes, Eileen Stevens, Reverend Tom Willis, Betty Saddler, Peggy Webb, Margaret Ashman, Brian Watson, Fred Meredith, Mary Ferguson, Steve Short, Anita Wain, Paul Wilson, Mark Ogden, Peter and Sarah Tomlinson, Paul Bonell, Pete Brennan, Roger Odd, Ann and Chris Bell, David Wilson, David Bowman and Lois Bowman, Joyce Baxter, Andrew Cook, Bill, Marjorie and Philip Daubney, Andrew Northern, Robert Curry and Paul Robinson.

THE STORY SO FAR.....

Or ghostly update, because that's what follows now.

Those familiar with our first collection will remember the story "Sounds from the night", when on two occasions about a year apart, a friend working at Westwood Hospital on night duty heard the sound of horses and noises that could be associated with stables. Initially his secret was shared only with us, that is until the publication of "Ghosts". This in turn led to a sequel, when another member of the hospital staff previously unaware of his colleague's experiences, until reading "Ghosts", revealed his own experiences at the Hospital whilst he had been on night duty. He also on two separate occasions, in the early hours of the morning, heard horses running past on the road outside, and thinking that it may be some that had escaped from the nearby stables in Pasture Terrace, went out to investigate, but was surprised on each occasion to find nothing!

And what did you think to the "Causeway Sprite"? For we are told there are others who have seen this strange apparition. One young lad whilst cycling along the Causeway had the mischievous imp follow him and the faster he pedalled, the quicker the Sprite moved, and only when a distance away from the Causeway did he realise 'it' had left him.

The mysteries of Well Lane still abound, as a young man discovered one night, whilst staying with his Grandparents in the lane. Peter was awakened when he felt the sensation of something on his bed, but as his Grandparents kept cats, he assumed one had walked across the bed. Peter settled down to go back to sleep, but the next thing he knew someone was getting into bed with him!

Feeling uneasy, he turned to look, and in the half light saw there next to him a young girl with blonde hair. Startled he leapt out of bed, quite unnerved by his unexpected bed mate, but then where was she? The bed was empty!!

In conversation, Peter mentioned the ghostly visitor to his Uncle, who surprised Peter by telling him that the same thing had happened to him previously in that very room!!

The Beverley Friary isn't without mention, for although there are

9

no new hauntings to report, we discovered others who did have ghostly visitors many years ago whilst living in the Friary. Remembering last time the disappointment we felt after speaking to an ex-resident who experienced nothing while living there, but wished she had, we were pointed in the direction of a 1957 newspaper. In its columns the question was asked "Is it haunted?"; this was the headline to a feature about the Friary and whether it had a ghost or not.

The report went on to tell of a workman who said he had seen a ghost in the garden; apparently he suddenly saw a dark figure near him, which made no sound or sign, then disappeared into 'thin air' leaving the workman in a 'distressed' condition. The story continues to tell of a daughter living at the Friary with her mother, the daughter went upstairs to her bedroom, a room noted for some ancient wooden panelling, she stood at one of the wardrobes tidying up some clothes inside, but on closing the door, she glanced to her left and saw a "shadowy figure" at the side of the wardrobe watching her. Fear struck the poor woman, she started to tremble and fled downstairs.

It appears Beverley's Historic Guildhall kept some of its secrets from us, that is until May 1988 when we were told of the following incidents that have taken place within the building.

It was during a conversation with Beverley's Mayor and Mayoress, Bill and Marjorie Daubney, that these mysteries were revealed. There are reports of footsteps being heard, and on two occasions they have caused concern. Once at a ladies' evening being held in the Mayor's Parlour, footsteps were heard as if walking below the floor level. The second time they were thought to be in the passage below, but again were somewhere between!!

Bill and Marjorie's son Philip had a more 'Hi Tech' experience, when using an autofocus video camera in the Parlour. The camera was firmly established on a tripod and was set focused on a static subject to be recorded, when quite suddenly the autofocus went completely haywire, varying the focus so dramatically that it was visibly noticeable on the lens barrel as it moved. Now on any autofocus camera, this only happens when the focal length varies, if someone or something moves within the lens range. On this occasion, no-one other than Philip was in the room, but 'something' caused that camera's autofocus to shift!! The drifting focus shows on the recording, but nothing unexpected appears. Bill went on to tell the story of one of the council's workmen who was carrying out repairs at the top of the stairs. When he saw a figure coming up the stairs towards the Mayor's Parlour, he spoke to the man, "Sorry Sir, you can't go in there; the Mayor's Parlour is closed". The man took no notice and continued to walk towards the parlour, apparently disappearing!

After completing his work on the ceiling and with strict instructions to leave the carpet clean, the workman went downstairs to find a brush in the old kitchen. There he came across an old man chopping sticks, the same man seen on the stairs. He asked if he could borrow a brush. The old man appeared oblivious to his presence and ignored him. Ruffled by the man's attitude, he helped himself to the brush, went back upstairs, cleaned up his mess and returned the brush.

When the caretaker came back, the workman asked who the old man was who wandered around, as he had seen him twice. The caretaker assured him that he had been the only person in the Guildhall and no-one else. With a chilling sensation he realised that when he had seen the old man come up the stairs, he had not climbed over the scaffolding as one had to, but had 'glided' through it, before disappearing through the door!

Still in the Guildhall and the Mayor's Parlour, this time it's Christmas 1987 and a family Christmas dinner, so much a family affair that even the dog was invited. During the meal, Bill felt the hair on the back of his neck "stand on end". Seconds later, the dog which had been asleep near the fire, suddenly jumped up and shot across the room and with its 'hackles' raised, stared intensely at the entrance door to the parlour. Bill calmed the dog saying "It's alright Rusty, don't get worried, it's only George, he won't harm you". The situation was repeated minutes later; as Bill felt his hair "stand on end" Rusty was again under the table, but staring, this time behind Bill.

So who is, or was George? Well it is thought to be the spirit of George Monkman, a past mace bearer, whose portrait hangs in the parlour and that the unrest may have been attributable to his portrait having been moved to the opposite end of the room!....

We are sure you will agree these experiences certainly add more support to the Guildhall hauntings.

And finally, the feather from the Ritz Cinema at Pocklington. This arrived in the post during March 1988 with a brief note explaining that it had been found in the Cinema. Now it's quite

11

possible this could have been brought in on someone's clothing, but remember Lynda who saw the strange "something" that flew across the auditorium then straight through the closed doors and the belief that during its history the loft had been used for the illegal sport of cock fighting? Need we say more?

Now, are you ready to join us on our next ghostly journey?.... You are?.... then read on....

MORE FROM THE PLAYHOUSE

It's not easy admitting to anyone that you've been haunted, seen a ghost or experienced the unexplained and even though I joined the other contributors and told my Playhouse stories I was apprehensive about revealing all, so I didn't and although the following may not be regarded as true hauntings in that sense, I feel they are covered under the heading of the unexplained. Now that we have a second collection, I have decided to include them.

Strong winds had dislodged some of the cinema's roof slates on the west side of the building and it wasn't until some rains came one Sunday morning that we realised our roof was leaking. Down it came, water poured in through two ceiling panels, bringing with it plaster. In due course the roof was made good and a local painter and decorator was called in to colour match the ceiling (a sort of nicotineic green) with the rest. His work was brilliant.

It wasn't long after this that two friends and myself, being staff and Film Society committee members, decided that it was time for a spring clean. We would wash the paintwork on the pillars, panels and plaques and freshen up the white paint with a re-coat. (Here I feel I should mention for those unfamiliar with the Playhouse, that on each wall pillar is a panel incorporating a plaque which I understand were imported from Italy during the early 1920's. These depict characters from Orpheus in the Underworld). As the Film Society became more established, we made every effort to 'tone down' the glossy bingo paint and, retaining the original colours, we carefully set about disposing of the gloss, introducing satin and matt finishes to give better distraction-free film viewing.

Steve and I had started the big wash down using mild detergent and hot water to remove the nicotine and dust from the paint. It was some time later we noticed the change. Soon after Andrew had

The Playhouse Cinema, Beverley.

13

started his white painting of the figures on the plaques, the background of each had been a bright gloss, wedgewood blue, but in the course of a few hours it changed to a wedgewood green!! They remain to this day untouched. Now this may not sound too unusual, until one looked up at the ceiling, only to see the plaque backgrounds had become a perfect colour match, I'm sure all these years on someone will have an explanation, but we found it quite uncanny, especially as the plaque in the foyer received the same treatment, but retained its original blue background!

Another strange event took place one morning while visiting the Westminster Bank. Leaving, I suddenly felt compelled to call at the Playhouse. Now I had no reason to go, but felt drawn to the place.

I unlocked the door and looked inside, everything appeared in order, and still I hadn't a clue why I was there, but seeing I was, I decided to have a quick look round. Upstairs in the office I soon discovered the reason for my visit. The air was full of blue smoke, on the electric cooker the milk pan had burnt dry, its bottom red hot! I switched the cooker off and opened a window; I now knew the reason for my visit!

Bingo had finished, leaving the usual mess of discarded Bingo books on the floor. Nightly, the staff checked each row of seats at the end of a session to ensure no burning cigarette ends remained and at the end of the evening before leaving the building a final check was often made, glancing down each row. On one such night, Adrian walked the east aisle, while I did the oppsite side, talking as we went. Suddenly Adrian stopped "I can't move" he said. "Stop messing about" was my reply, "No, honest, I can't move" and sure enough he couldn't. He went on to say that he had walked into a cold spot and could move neither forward or backwards. If I hadn't seen it I would never had believed it.

Although his inanimate state didn't last for long, it seemed like an age to me. Later as we reflected on the incident, we both admitted that we had noticed "cold spots" before, but never given them any thought!

Again in Bingo days, I experienced a similar occurence. One night shortly before leaving for home, I felt as though there was something behind me. I shivered and felt cold. Looking behind, there was nothing to see, but I felt as though ice was being run down my back. It was unpleasant and I was afraid. I locked up, left and walked home all the time feeling as though something was behind me. Only

14

on reaching my front door and turning the key did I feel free again.

The following night I decided that whatever had frightened me, I would try to face and so in the empty building I sat until a few minutes past midnight, waiting - but to my relief there was no repeat performance.

I feel this incident that took place in early 1988 may have been a case of one good turn deserving of another, the first good turn being that of the pan left on the cooker.

About 45 minutes of film were left before the end, the projectionist had noticed the strong smell of something electrical overheating and as on previous occasions it had come from the rectifier (this is a large box full of things for converting the mains A.C. current into D.C. to ignite and run the projector's lamp).

Over a few months many checks had been made on the rectifier and servicing carried out to eliminate the smell which was usually caused by connections in need of a clean or having vibrated loose.

On this particular night, I passed the projection box on my way to the office and commented to the projectionist that the smell was back, and at the same time thought 'we shall have to get in touch with the electrician again'. I decided to take a look and sniff around; the cause of the smell was very much in evidence, a connection was overheating and glowing red hot. I called our electrician who agreed to come and have a look. If all was safe we could continue as I desperately wanted to avoid shutting down the show having visions of a near riot from the youngsters who formed a threequarters-full house.

The electrician advised trying to cool the affected contact, and this we did using a small fan. Duly the electrician arrived and confirmed we had a big problem, but felt there was no immediate danger, so with care and supervision we could manage to run to the end of the show, of which by this time only about 15 minutes remained.

I always feel there is help somewhere nearby in the Playhouse, so in a moment alone I spoke my thoughts aloud and asked for help to resolve the problem, or see us through to the end of the film.

Over the following minutes the electrician made repeated checks on the equipment and explained what was happening, then after one of his checks he came back and stared straight at me and said "The Gods are on your side tonight". My puzzled look brought forth an explanation - quite suddenly that hot contact had cooled dramatically and the meter levels dropped indicating the power was now flowing normally. Thankfully the show ended flawlessly.

The following morning the electrician carried out the necessary repairs.

Well, what do you think, was it a coincidence or could it have been a return favour?

PHR

Away now from my unexplained experiences at the Playhouse and on to that of one of our projectionists, who by coincidence shares the same birthday as the cinema, February 20th.

Paul had just returned to the projection box to ensure everything was running smoothly when he heard above the sound of the projector a voice saying "good focus". Thinking that it was Paul, the Assistant Manager, he looked to where he had expected him to be to make the comment, but there was no-one there. Somewhat curious, Paul immediately checked both the office and adjacent areas, but found no-one; then he thought it must have come over on the intercom, so he contacted the paybox, the only other station on the intercom. He was assured that he had not been called since the show had begun.

So who would you think that voice belonged to? We have a good idea, as those of you who are by now fully conversant with the Playhouse stories surely will!!

THE KINGS HEAD HOTEL

For those not familiar with Beverley, the Kings Head Hotel is situated in the town's Saturday Market Place and, as well as providing hotel accommodation, boasts a superb restaurant, and at the time of writing two attractive and popular bars.

During the early eighties, alterations and improvements took place, the results of which are as presented in 1988. During the renovation, the little shop next door (previously an "off licence", second-hand selling service and before that a well established butcher's shop) was acquired and became part of the Kings Head.

It is behind the shop area that a mysterious man has been seen. He

16

The Kings Head Hotel, Beverley.

was first noticed late one evening, Paul the manager had secured the premises for the night and switched off all the tills, but then as an afterthought decided to check that the till in the restaurant, one easily forgotten, was also off. Paul left the bar passing through double doors into the restaurant foyer. Turning right he saw to his surprise, the figure of a man leaning against the old fire place. Wondering who it was, and what he was doing there, he wasted no time in approaching the stranger, but in the seconds it took to get there, his view of "him" was obscured momentarily by a pillar, but sufficiently long enough for the man to have disappeared, the room being completely empty! Later Paul reflected on the incident and became convinced that what he had seen must have been a ghost! But of whom? Though facially he was not distinguishable, his clothes were reminiscent of a 1930's farm-hand!

Our story does not end yet, for as well as other staff being aware of his presence, having sensed, and felt as though someone was there, but not, a waitress going about her duties suddenly saw a customer she hadn't noticed before. She reached for a menu, turned round to pass it to him, but was astonished to find he had gone. Adding to the mystery was the fact that there was no way he could have left the room without his walking past her!

However, a possible solution as to who the Kings Head ghost may be came to light when a local newspaper, the Beverley Star, carried a feature on the town's public houses. Apparently some years ago the Kings Head restaurant had been the sight of the stalls belonging to the old Pack Horse Inn, the very place where it is understood a soldier took his own life. We wonder, could the stranger who appears in tweeds be this same unfortunate man?

LOVE... AND MURDER!

Although this is not a ghost story, it is true, and tells of a tragedy that may have a degree of relevance to hauntings in certain parts of Beverley.

The year was 1857, the month October. Helen, aged 31, had been in service as housemaid to Mr John Maister of Register Square for six years. Henry, aged about 34, was Mr Maister's gardener, a widower with three children. Using that romantic Victorian term, Helen and Henry were "sweethearts". But this was an obsessive romance, Henry wanted to marry Helen, but circumstances around Henry's nephew, and his apprenticeship at the iron foundry, held her back from marriage.

Cross words were often exchanged, accompanied by fits of rage from Henry. It was known on one occasion he threatened to hang himself in the greenhouse and is understood to have produced a suitable handkerchief for the purpose.

Although unable to assess the date of the tragedy accurately, it was reported in the Beverley Guardian that it was believed the crime was committed sometime between the hours of two and five in the afternoon, but the bodies were not discovered until midnight. You see it was thought that whilst in a fit of rage, Henry killed Helen and then tried to take his own life.

Now if you are faint hearted, then read no further.

Helen was found "stiff and cold", her throat having been cut from "ear to ear". Henry was found a couple of yards away, face down. It was thought he too was dead, but when turned over, he was still breathing. His throat was also cut, but by his own hand.

Pools of blood were on the footpath and nearby hedge. It was later thought that Henry had committed his deed elsewhere in the garden and removed Helen's body to the place where she was found, which was under an apple tree, laying with her head resting in the artichokes.

(The reader may be interested to know that until a few years ago, before County Hall was extensively altered, there were several very old apple and pear trees still growing and bearing fruit in the area where we believe John Maister's garden to have been situated. Perhaps it was one of those very trees under which the unfortunate Helen's body was found?)

Henry, very weak, was moved to Mr Maister's house and the surgeon sent for. Helen was removed to the stable.

A suicide note was found on a slate, which was later identified as being in Henry's writing. This was confirmed by his nephew.

Henry lingered in agony for twelve days. One report on the state of his health read as follows:

> "Still alive, but gradually sinking, the greater part
> of the nourishment administered to him coming out
> again through the wound in the throat, instead of
> passing into the stomach."

Recovery was sufficient for Henry to be moved to his house in Well Lane, and there he showed signs of improvement, but the prospect of the gallows ahead made him beg the medical attendants to let him die. Tubes were used in an effort to feed him, but repeatedly he bit them; probably a combination of his injury and lack of nourishment brought about his death.

The press coverage of Henry's funeral on November 5th, is reproduced as reported:

> "shortly before twelve o'clock, the remains of the
> wretched man were interred without funeral service
> in the midst of a numerous assemblage of spectator,
> the only light being from a few candles and the
> watchman's lanterns, and from the dense fog which
> prevailed at the time, the scene was gloomy indeed,
> and seemed to correspond with the melancholy
> tragedy."

19

Love and Murder.

I was curious to know if any record of this burial existed, but research proved negative. Henry was just one of hundreds buried in the Minster graveyard. You may now wonder why this story has been included. Well, I think it may be possible that one of those Well Lane hauntings could be attributed to Henry! Who knows? It's just a thought, and as for poor Helen, it has been said that Register Square is haunted by the ghost of a woman.

PHR

BEVERLEY PUBLIC LIBRARY

During the last War when people had to spend nights in the library on fire watch, it is said that no-one would stay in the reference section, the reason being that sounds of people and things moving were heard, when there was no-one to be seen!

But who knows? With that vast richness of life within those old newspapers, possibly those 'pages from the past' may have been on the turn!!!

THE FIRST FLOOR VISITOR

The property this story originates from is within a stone's throw of Beverley's Lairgate and its already recorded hauntings. The teller has asked to remain anonymous.

Mid-summer 1981 and Andrew's parents were away on holiday leaving him and his sister in care of the house. Andrew had during this week seized the opportunity to stay up late watching TV.

In fact it was in the early hours of the Thursday morning when he finally decided to go to bed, and whilst laying there waiting for the curtain of sleep to fall, he saw appear through the bedroom wall a ghostly looking figure. "Mesmerised" with fear, Andrew stared as the figure of a woman in long skirt and bonnet glided across the room disappearing through the opposite wall. Needless to say that visitation afforded Andrew no sleep for the rest of that night.

Later, confiding in his mother, he was allowed to change bedrooms for a while with his sister, but the secret being kept from her, that is until quite some time after. On later hearing of her brother's experience, she then told of the happening in the house next door but one, where her friend lived, for she too had witnessed

The First Floor Visitor.

what appeared to be the same ghostly woman pass through her bedroom.

Strange as this coincidence may sound, it doesn't end here, for when new neighbours arrived next door, it is understood that their youngest son had seen something in his bedroom, for he was afraid to return there.

Odd isn't it that this ghostly woman has appeared in three separate properties, each time on the first floor level, within a radius of 50 metres!

It has been said this visitor could be the ghost of a poor woman who was drowned many years ago in the town ditch which once flowed in the vicinity of those houses.

Steve
Oldfield
1988

The Monks Walk.

THE MONKS WALK

The present name of this public house is believed to originate from the passageway which runs from the front to the rear of the building, which during the plagues of the 1600's was used by monks to carry victims of the plague through to the burial pits (known as the trinities) under what is now the Railway Station and old coal yard.

The monks have long since gone. The name now being the only reminder of this grim association......or is it?

Sheila and Phil Harrison took over the Monks Walk in July 1986 giving little, if any, thought to its previous history; having heard the pub was haunted we asked Phil if he could confirm it, and this he did.

They had only been in the place a week when their first suspicions of a possible haunting occurred; each morning for a whole week, they found a half pint glass of lager had been pulled and left standing on the window sill behind the fruit machine. This caused sufficient concern for them to consider staying there; was it possible they had missed this glass while clearing up? No; a thorough check had been made every night, yet a glass of lager was there each morning for that week.

The next incident occurred several weeks later. Phil was in the cellar when without warning the lights and power failed. During this period of darkness a white, featureless figure appeared about six foot in front of him and drifted slowly across the cellar towards the door. The power returned and Phil left the cellar somewhat hastily. Although not sure of what he had seen, it was soon confirmed the pub had a ghost.

Sometime later Sheila and Phil were having a farewell drink with a friend who was leaving to join the Navy; it was during this private celebration they had another "visitor". Nothing was to be seen, but there was the sound of chains or keys being shaken accompanied by a distinct coldness and gaseous smell. The sounds moved from the restaurant area out through a nearby door, down the outside passage, back through the door at the front, trailing off into the restaurant! This incident was sufficient to cause their friend to depart in haste!

Sheila and Phil appear to have settled well, and although Phil has seen 'his' featureless apparition again, neither he nor Sheila are unduly concerned with their hauntings.

MORE MONKS

We are quite surprised by the number of ghostly monks that have been seen in Beverley and are somewhat puzzled by their appearances. After all as men of the Church, surely they would have been at peace with the world in both life and death, so why do they continue to haunt? We have no explanation.

If you are already aware of the monks from the Friary, Armstrongs and Chantry Lane, permit us to introduce some more.

During the 1920's, Florrie's father worked at the Tannery. One night he worked late to complete an urgent order and it was in the early hours of the morning that he walked home past the north side of the Minster.

Nearing what is now the parish rooms, though formerly the site of a hospital for the monks, he saw two figures leaving the doors of the Minster; both were dressed in black and proceeded to cross the road to the rooms. Courteously, Florrie's father bid them the time of night, to which there was no reply. He suddenly realised he had just spoken to two ghostly monks.

While Jack was fighting for his country, his wife lived in a caravan on the south side of the Minster in Baxter's field, behind which was located a small jail, its purpose being to hold prisoners overnight who were on route to larger establishments.

On one particular evening, Jack's wife went out to collect water. It was whilst doing this chore that she saw a monk clothed in black; so close was the figure and it appeared very real to her. Realising it was a ghost, she fled in fear, never daring to return to that place again!

More Monks.

25

LONG LANE

Living in Beverley's Keldgate, Adrian used Long Lane as a short cut on many occasions, when driving home from Hull.

On one such occasion, the lane was shrouded in darkness, which so often accompanies this type of tale, creating an air of eeriness.

On this night he was returning home when quite suddenly he saw a "shape" move across the road in front of his car. He braked feeling sure beyond doubt that this was no near miss. He had definitely hit something, either human or animal.

Filled with fear and panic, he jumped out of the car expecting to face some terrible tragedy, but there was nothing in front, under or behind the car.

Shaken, he continued on home and since then has been reluctant to use the lane.

Sometime later, a family friend told of the night she was travelling alone along the same lane, when in roughly the same place, she saw a woman at the roadside. Thinking the woman might want a lift to Beverley, she stopped; upon doing so the rear door opened and the stranger got in closing the door behind her. About to drive away, she glanced in her rear view mirror, to see no-one there. The passenger had gone, without even a word of thanks!!

THE LORD NELSON

Occupying number 13 Flemingate, Beverley, is the Lord Nelson public house which is believed to have been established on this site as early as 1620.

Although thought to have had an unblemished history, it is not without a 'presence'. Footsteps have been heard to walk across the bar floor, but more substance for the 'presence' comes from Joanne Kilburn, who at the time of writing lives in part of the 1st floor. Joanne says she often becomes aware of a 'something' being there, usually heralded when her dog becomes 'anxious' and will not settle. Joanne admits that frequently she has felt as though she were being watched almost to the point of supervision, and that if she were to do something wrong, she would be corrected.

Even her infant child of 5 months wakes up practically every morning in the early hours, often quite distressed, but when the child sleeps anywhere other than at the Lord Nelson, the night's rest is unbroken!

Strange, but true.

WAS IT JUST A DREAM?

When we first heard of a haunting from a property near the trinities, Beverley, we anticipated hearing a story associated with the plague victims of the 17th Century, who were buried under what is now the railway station.

Initially we were disappointed to discover it wasn't, but it did provide us with an insight into an interesting experience.

The property formed part of an old farm house believed at one time to be the residence of a dairy owner.

Was it Just a Dream?

Sixteen years ago Jackie was living in this house with her parents. One night comfortable in her bed, she was awakened by the sound of someone walking across her bedroom. Jackie was petrified as she saw an old man with a peculiar shaped nose, limp across from one door to the other dragging what looked like a crippled or injured foot. She was unable to scream, the silence being broken only by the sound of her heart thumping in her ears. The old man then disappeared through the other door.

Although frightened at the time, Jackie thought afterwards it was really no more than a bad dream.

However, two years later, her bedroom, now in what had once been a large pantry, was to be the site of yet another "bad dream", or was it?

Jackie was awakened only to see that same man again sitting on the end of her bed. Hoping it was no more than a dream, she closed her eyes tight, moments later opened them again, and was terrified to see him sat next to her. She reached out to touch him, but her hand passed straight through him. As he disappeared Jackie heard a voice say "why?"

Although there is no certainty, it has been thought that Jackie's visitor may have been that one time dairy owner...or was it just a dream.....?

TRINITY LANE

When I first heard this story, I couldn't help but wonder how many readers would remember dancing the night away at the old Hodgson's Ballroom in Priory Road. Of the many functions I attended there, one feature prominent in my memory was that floor and its incredible springiness. Anyway, enough of my ramblings and on with the story.

Terry, like so many Beverley folk frequented Hodgson's Ball-room. On that particular night after the dance, he had taken a girl to her home in Highgate. On his return walk, he crossed Eastgate, past the Oddfellows public house and into Trinity Lane. When having walked only the short distance past the Masonic Hall and just before the road forks, Terry noticed a shadowy figure moving towards him from his left. "It" brushed past him disappearing into the wall of the large warehouse type building near to the Telegraph public house.

Realising he had just seen a ghost, Terry ran the rest of the way home, it being a considerable time before he dared to venture that way again.

I am left wondering and daring to presume that the "shadowy figure" may have been a ghostly monk. "It" crossed the road from left to right or virtually North to South, possibly heading in the direction of the Friary.

Monks were very much involved in the care of plague victims, that being so it's worth noting that during the plague of 1610 a pest house was established on a site on or near to what is now the Railway Station, within a stone's throw of Terry's apparition. So is it possible that Terry's ghost may have been some poor old monk from all those years past returning to the Friary?

PHR

A WINTER'S NIGHT

Although not sure of the actual month, Kathie does remember for certain that it was a winter's night and snowing, the snow having formed a substantial covering on the roads and footpaths sufficient to make them quite hazardous.

Kathie and her friend Julie, had left work and headed for home. Walking along Goths Lane, Kathie noticed a lady she knew walking ahead and pushing a cycle with bags hanging from the handlebars. Kathie thought how sensible she was not trying to ride her cycle on a night like that. The lady turned off Goths Lane, as Kathie and friend continued to its end.

Calling at a shop before going home, Kathie was told the sad news about that same lady who had that morning taken her own life, "It's not true" said Kathie, "I've just seen her, Julie and I have walked behind her down Goths Lane!"

Kathie knew she had seen this person, recognising her by her walk, clothes and being only a matter of feet away, and said she had not made a mistake! But sadly that lady who Kathie saw had ended her life tragically that morning.

MILL LANE

In our first collection we told of the "unfortunate accident" that is believed to have happened in Mill Lane, Beverley; from that same lane comes another story, this time of a haunted property.

It was thought that the strange things that happened may have been brought about as the result of internal structural alterations.

The first incident occurred one night. Wendy was awakened by a burning sensation on her cheek, and upon opening her eyes, was horrified to see the vague figure of a person, later thought to have been a man, reaching out and touching her face. Frightened to say the least, she woke her husband and explained what had happened only seconds earlier; he saw nothing.

The following day the night's experience was very much in evidence. The burning she had felt now manifested itself in the shape of four finger like marks across her cheek. Being concerned, Wendy visited her doctor, who told he that he thought the marks were attributable to her having been touched by someone with shingles!!

But Wendy knew she had not. Two nights later and sleeping on the other side of the bed, the figure of the person appeared briefly to her again, but this time, thankfully there was no contact.

However, Wendy was not the only one to see the "figure", for about a week later her 'middle' son said he too had seen "it" on the landing.

Afraid more for her young family than herself, Wendy persuaded her husband to put the house on the market, but in view of Wendy expecting again and having earlier lost a baby, her Doctor advised against the move until after the birth.

In the mean time, a pungent smell of cigar smoke randomly permeated different rooms throughout the house without explanation. Also bumps were heard one night, thought by the 'middle son' to be his parents going down stairs. Curious he went to have a look and found at the bottom of the stairs a pile of books which he subsequently got the blame for, but he was not guilty!

After about a month, the "finger marks" cleared from Wendy's cheek, but she was left feeling very uneasy when she discovered that some time previously an old man had lived in the same house and had died as a result of contracting shingles!!

A sinister story indeed, and to the best of our knowledge this is the only story we have come across where a ghostly contact has left a physical mark.

THE REGAL

I have been told that the Regal, now incorporating the old Assembly rooms, at the corner of Manor Road and Norwood had a ghostly presence. In fact I have a vague recollection of being told that 'it' used to walk across the Ballroom floor.

Some people are rumoured to have 'seen' and 'felt' a presence in various parts of the building, including one gentleman who has seen and spoken to "something", while others think the 'chills' they have felt are no more than variations in air pressure when doors open and close.

However, it is believed that the 'ghost' originates from an unfortunate man who fell to his death whilst the building was being constructed. One source says that it happened in the 1760's when the Assembly rooms were built, whilst another claims it happened during the conversion to a cinema in 1935. My researches have found nothing in the way of a tragedy associated with the building, but I did discover the Assembly rooms were extended in 1840, so who knows what happened then?

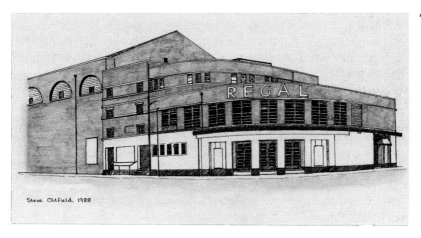

Steve Oldfield 1988

The Regal, Beverley.

The record of the Regal hauntings you have just read was, I felt, a bit disappointing and so was removed from the first collection of stories. But even though some explained certain happenings as little more than changes in air pressure, I still remembered the tale being told of something walking the Ballroom floor, so you can imagine my delight when told the following incident.

PHR

It was one of the General Elections in the Seventies. The Regal Ballroom was the designated collection point for the Ballot boxes and the subsequent count. As will be appreciated, security was required to protect the boxes. On this occasion the two guards were a police constable and the teller of this story, Tom, who had during election day acted as a returning officer.

Secure in the building and as comfortable as is possible in sleeping bags, Tom and his colleague settled down for the night.

Sometime during the early hours, Tom and the policeman were suddenly awakened by the sound of footsteps walking across the floor. The only illumination coming into the room was from the street lights in Manor Road, casting a dim, eerie glow across the floor. The footsteps 'walked' the full length of the ballroom from entrance door to the stage. The concerned and somewhat nervous observers saw no-one. On reaching the stage the tone of the footfalls changed as they climbed up the side stairs and walked across the stage, here sounding more hollow. They then terminated in an almighty crash; as Tom said it was as though someone had "hit a thunder sheet or something"!

The policeman went immediately to investigate the origin of the crash, but found no-one or anything that could have caused the noise.

A search of the building was made, everything was found to be in order, leaving open the question of who walked the floor that night!!

NORWOOD

Further along Norwood are two houses where strange happenings have occurred. The first one we have called "The Shadow past the windows". The house has to remain anonymous, the story coming by way of a relative of a one-time occupant.

The house used to have two windows down its side leading to a rear door, and forming a passageway with the opposite wall. This sets the scene for "the shadow".

Various members of the family whilst in the room would notice a shadow pass the first and then the second window, leading them to believe that at any moment there would be a knock on the door. In anticipation, one of them would move to "answer" the door which on these occasions revealed no-one. However, this shadow was not just restricted to the family, as friends are also known to have seen it.

While leaving the house one night, a relative passed someone on the pathway at the side of the house. 'He' was walking towards the back door.

The following morning she enquired about the late night visitor by making 'tongue in cheek' comments, only to discover that no-one had called at the house after she left.

THE OLD LADY OF NORWOOD

Another house in Beverley's Norwood has on numerous occasions given its occupants an unnerving chill or two. We don't intend to reveal the house number, just in case its present occupants haven't discovered the old lady yet.

The story was told by a lady who lived in the house for two years and had never really settled in it. However on the Friday before she and her husband were due to leave on the Monday, she was in the house with a friend when quite suddenly they both heard the sound of someone walking along the passageway, this being particularly noticeable as the carpets had been taken up for the move. The footsteps continued up the stairs causing them to creak as they moved.

The lady occupant was too frightened to move, but her friend grabbed the poker and bravely went in pursuit of the intruder, but to her surprise there was no-one there. The following day the neighbours were asked if they had heard anything, but their answer was negative.

Over the next few years the house came on the market several times, no-one appearing to stay there very long. In the early eighties the house was for sale again, so the original occupant who tells this tale was curious to know if the house was haunted and to see if "anything had happened". It wasn't long before she came into conversation with the seller, not revealing that she too had once lived there. Eventually the question was asked "is this place haunted?" The answer was "Yes", but this wasn't the reason for them leaving. They had experienced a rocking chair rocking by itself and strong smells of "real old fashioned perfume", and on one occasion all the furniture had been "moved around". However, the experiences had been recorded by others who had lived in and visited the house.

It's believed possible that the "happenings" could have been the result of an old lady who had once lived and died in the house.

LADY-LE-GROS

We had heard murmerings about strange things happening at the Lady-Le-Gros at the east end of Norwood, but hadn't got around to researching the story when a report of the "ghostly goings-on" appeared in the Beverley Guardian on February 25th 1988. This prompted us to investigate this story for ourselves.

Research proves that a Beerhouse has existed on or near to the present site for a great many years. In fact the original building pre dates 1873, when it was first named the Lady-Le-Gros. The 'Beer Seller' or Landlord was also a cow keeper by the name of Samuel Peacock. It is also said that a clay pipe factory dating back to Napoleonic days was probably situated in the same area, this being established by a great number of fragments being unearthed over a period of years.

Pete and Jenny took over the Lady-Le-Gros on December 7th 1987. A small party was held on the transition of landlords, photographs being taken. When processed, one photo showed on the wall, the face of what was thought to be that of a cavalier.

However, Pete and the regulars dismissed it as nothing more than the flash light effect on patterned wallpaper and one regular in particular, who usually occupied a seat at the end of the bar, openly scoffed at the "Cavalier" suggestion. Even when the light bulb near his head exploded and a horse brass nearly fell on him, he remained undaunted, as did the new landlord and the pub's regulars.

Christmas and the New Year afforded the new tenants the chance to settle, that is until one night. Pete had been serving, when he had to visit the cellar to change barrels. The operation was completed

34

The Lady Le Gros.

with ease, but he soon discovered a vacuum in the delivery pipe attributable to the tap for the carbon dioxide gas supply being switched off. Now the strange thing was, if this had been switched off earlier in the evening, he would have noticed, as there would have been no beer delivery to the bar.

Pete's first thoughts were that a member of the darts team, who had left minutes previously, had gone down into the cellar and turned the gas off for a joke. Upon their return Pete expected some comments from them about a pub with no beer, but as there were no 'cracks' to this effect, he asked if any of them had touched the taps in the cellar - none had.

The situation was to repeat itself several times until the staff began to keep a vigilant eye on the cellar door, ensuring that no unauthorised personnel had access. Still no explanation could be found for the gas taps being switched off. The mystery deepened when one night the taps were switched on and the central heating clock was altered throwing the timing sequence completely out.

The number of times the gas taps have been interfered with has ruled out any possibility of an accidental cause and as Pete showed us, it takes a very positive movement to switch them 'on' and 'off'.

A general feeling of unease now exists. So much so that Pete's son refuses to go down to the cellar and the bar man will not go down unaccompanied. So just who or what is behind this remains a mystery!!!

CLOISTERS

Situated at the North Bar Within end of Tiger Lane, one finds a charming restaurant known as the Cloisters.

The building dates from 1730 and was at that time known as the Tiger Inn, until the late 1840's when, with the advent of the railway, it ceased business as a coaching inn; the building was separated into shops and is still so to this day with of course the exception of Cloisters.

Up until the late seventies, this site had been a motor spares store for Armstrong's Garage just across Tiger Lane and now St Mary's Court. It is said that many of the mechanics from the garage often felt uneasy at going into the store and one poor chap in particular refused totally to enter the premises unaccompanied after dark, hence the place acquiring a reputation for being haunted.

Armstrong's eventually moved to a new site, the stores becoming the White Rabbit second-hand bookshop.

Next came the wine bar originally known as Upstairs, Downstairs, but before opening it underwent extensive alterations. During this upgrading, a young joiner was working on the top floor when somebody touched him on the shoulder. He spun round to meet whoever it was, but saw no-one. This experience unsettled him so much, he refused to work there alone again. The work took over a year to complete and during this time the aforementioned incident repeated itself, this time on the ground floor where the recipient was a bricklayer. This resulted in work being held up for a week, continuing only after a great deal of persuasion to entice him back.

During the summer of 1982, the wine bar, having been open several months, had the need for the services of a joiner, and whilst working on the staircase between the ground and first floor, his apprentice saw at the top of the stairs the head and shoulders of a blonde haired boy with a scarf around his neck!!

Other happenings in the restaurant have involved a heavy door situated along the side of the entrance hallway, that frequently and inexplicably opens accompanied by a whistling sound, seen and heard by several people. Gas bottles have often been turned off when they should have been on, and vice versa; a plant pot appeared to 'jump' from the shelf to the floor! And a former manageress reported seeing a bunch of keys slide along the length of the bar!

Steve Oldfield 1988

Cloisters.

37

Then there was the Sunday morning, about 1.30 a.m. when the owner heard the most unearthly sounds seemingly from upstairs, as if something was being dragged across the floor, but at the same time thinking it may be something in the lane outside, checked to find nothing. However, sometime later the owner received a call from his wife who had been locking up the premises. She too had heard sounds from upstairs, fearing an intruder. This time the police were called. Interestingly enough the officers sent to investigate had been told most seriously that the premises were reported to be haunted! And of course the subsequent search revealed no-one.

Well, here we have another of those hauntings without explanation, but we found it interesting and you may too when you learn that the majority of the interior furnishings originated from an old church in Hull!

PEEL PLACE

Peel Place is just on the left of North Bar Without, a few yards past the Rose and Crown public house.

Peel Place.

Having left the Regal Ballroom one night after a dance, a lady resident of Peel Place was returning home; turning from North Bar Without, she entered the arched area, and ahead saw a man in a top hat looking very old fashioned.

He walked towards her and she towards him; he made no offer to move from her intended path; she thought to herself that she wouldn't move for him and didn't, for as she drew closer, he disappeared only to re-appear behind her continuing his walk. It was almost as though she had walked through him. Feeling 'uncomfortable' to say the least, she wasted no time getting indoors.

A FISHY TALE....

....Was told to me many years ago; in fact I had completely forgotten it, that is until a friend reminded me of the people and their fisherman friend.

The house on Hillcrest Drive, Beverley was occupied by a family of three: mother, father and young daughter. Sadly the mother has died but years earlier told us of their ghostly happenings; from memory my friend and I both recall that their ghostly visitor was a fisherman dressed in oilskins, his presence invariably being heralded by the strong smell of fish.

On the occasions he did appear, it was at the top of the stairs on the landing. We understand all three members of the family experienced this visitor, but could afford no explanation to his origins.

PHR

SNOW GHOST!

From Molescroft Beverley, we heard the following story.

The view from the window was as picturesque as many a Christmas card; the trees and garden shrubs bowed under the weight of the night's snow. It was then the teller noticed the thick blanket of snow covering his car, and contemplated the road conditions for the journey that lay ahead. Still he lingered a few moments longer, taking in that winter scene, especially as the snow lay undisturbed.

The Snow Ghost.

In due course, he ventured outside to clear the snow from his car. While doing this, a passerby, well wrapped up against the cold, walked past and entered into an exchange of words about the weather. His car cleared he looked round, and was suddenly aware that the person he had just spoken to had left no footprints in the snow; only his own were round the car, and glancing up the road the snow still lay undisturbed, that passerby nowhere in sight!!

COWBOY

When I read this story, I could plainly hear the voice of its author in my mind, so it was decided that this story had to be included as originally written, but I'm sure you will agree it is a wonderfully personal story. So now let me introduce you to "Cowboy".

PHR

After the birth of my first child, I found I was pregnant again. Unfortunately, I miscarried. I instinctively knew this was a boy, although it had never been medically proved to me. However, within the first month of the miscarriage happening, my daughter started having an imaginary friend who stayed with her for what was to become years and years, and in fact still visits now in her sixteenth year. At first I took her to the doctor, who said she was lonely. I found this difficult to believe as the house was always full of children her own age; however he insisted she went to a full time nursery. Instead of taking her mind off this imaginary friend, she now called "Cowboy", the situation got worse. She would insist "Cowboy" went with her to nursery and in the evening give me a 'blow by blow' account of everything she and Cowboy had done. I took all this with a pinch of salt, assuming that as time went on, she would grow out of it. She never did.

By the time she was eleven years old, Cowboy had become one of the family. A few times I thought she was a crazy child, until one day I read a magazine article on Doris Stokes who said that miscarried children often returned to the earth's plane and latched onto a brother or sister; still sceptical, I approached my eleven year old daughter and asked her to describe Cowboy to me in detail, which she did: she also told me he came to her now in times of trouble or upset; she told me of his blond curly hair, his features, dress etc.

With all this knowledge tucked inside me, I wasn't sure what to do. I left it for two years or so, then came the death of my father who had been ill in hospital; the night before he died, he told us how well he was feeling; I came home and told my daughter that Grandad was so much better he was coming home the next morning.

At a quarter to four in the morning the following day, the telephone rang to say Dad had taken a turn for the worse. I dashed upstairs to get ready, only to find my daughter sat on the edge of her bed telling me Cowboy was with her; he had come this time to take Grandad off. She said Cowboy was going now and Grandad would be happy. I was stunned; the telephone rang again, this time to tell me it was too late, he had died; the uncanny thing is it was at exactly the same time as Cowboy was going.

Six months after the death of my father, I went to a spiritualist who said my father was with a boy whom he called "Sunshine boy". When I asked her to describe him it was as exactly as my daughter had described him earlier. She told me how this boy had collected

41

Dad and how he was looking after him now.

My daughter still sees Cowboy occasionally, mainly when she is troubled or upset: she said he comforts her and protects her.

WHODUNNIT?

This is not a ghost story or even the smallest of hauntings, but we did find it to be an interesting and intriguing mystery from 1853, which we feel worthy of inclusion.

Within the Beverley Minster Churchyard, a stone marks the last resting place of Caroline Duffill, upon which was inscribed a curious epitaph, now illegible through the ravages of time. Thankfully the original wording had been preserved in the church records and reads as follows:

> Caroline, wife of Thomas Duffill
> who departed this life,
> the 24th January 1853.
> Aged 38 years.

> "Mysterious was my cause of death in the prime of life I fell. For days I lived yet never had breath, the secret of my fate to tell. Farewell my child and husband dear, by cruel hands I leave You, now that I'm dead and sleeping here, my murderer may deceive You. Though I am dead, yet shall I live, I must my murderer meet, and then in evidence shall give my cause of death complete. Forgive my child and husband dear, that cruel man of blood. He soon for murder must appear Before the Son of God".

We are aware many people have heard of, or about, this so called tombstone. We had hoped to solve the mystery behind the wording, but no such luck! The secret has been taken to the grave.

However, the events leading up to Caroline's death fuel the mystery even more.

She spent that winter's afternoon in Hull with her Aunt Catherine

42

Judge and during the course of the afternoon they had met with William Halliday, a cow keeper from Beverley. After a few drinks, but not to excess, it was soon time for Caroline to leave for Beverley, catching the last train back.

Halliday joined her in the second class compartment, to which Caroline expressed her displeasure by asking her Uncle James Judge, to accompany her to Beverley. He declined saying she would be alright with Halliday.

It is not known whether anything happened between Hull and Cottingham, but as the train left Cottingham station, a porter who happened to be in a position to see all the carriages pass by, saw Caroline put her head out of the door window and yell "Thief, thief!" followed by the appearance of a hand on the door handle.

The porter shouted at them to sit down and leave the door alone, but a moment later he saw someone fall from the carriage. The porter ran along the track whereupon he found the poor Caroline laid on the railway sidings with a severeley cut head and in an incoherent state.

When the train arrived at Beverley, the compartment door was found to be open, but the compartment empty! It was later confirmed that Halliday had jumped from the train as it approached the station. The incident was fully investigated by Mr Hawker, the Superintendent of the York and North Midland Railway, who eventually arrested Halliday.

Meanwhile, the day after the incident Caroline's husband Thomas brought her home to the Freemasons Arms. Sadly she never regained consciousness, dying a few days later. Halliday was sent to the York assizes charged with manslaughter.

So was Caroline pushed or did she jump? At the inquiry the porter had stated that he could not be sure if the hand on the door handle was that belonging to a man or woman!

By now you too must be wondering what relevance the wording of that epitaph has in relation to the actual incident, since the aforementioned evidence identifies the culprit, whereas the epitaph appears to indicate other possibilities, and furthermore who worded it?

HAUNTINGS FROM HULL

A NIGHT AT THE PICTURES!

For those unfamiliar with the Central Library in Hull's Albion Street, there is, besides reading matter, a wealth of film entertainment at the Hull Film Theatre. This is a 249 seat cinema tucked away within the library complex. From behind the scenes comes our next story.

For many years Peter had been interested in the acquisition and collection of films of local historical interest. His enthusiasm for the subject and love of the cinema overflowed not only to his family, but many friends who had the privilege and pleasure of sharing Peter's hobby. This interest had also afforded Peter the position of a projectionist in the Film Theatre's team.

Tragically after a short illness, Peter passed on and sadly with him a wealth of cinematic knowledge was lost.

It was during a show that the new projectionist, Jamie, felt a "presence pass through him" and at the same time saw a person's "shadow" appear on the wall in front, but what startled him was the sudden appearance on the wall of white lettering spelling out the name Margaret!

Later after the show Jamie told his story to the Duty Manager, who happened to be a close friend of the deceased. He then learned that Peter's widow had been in the audience that night, her first visit to the Film Theatre since her husband's death; her name ... Margaret!

THE PROSPECT CENTRE

Across the road from the Central Libary and Film Theatre, is the Prospect Street shopping centre, now occupying the site of the old Hull Royal Infirmary. Prior to that, the area was known as Whiting's Field, where numerous public executions took place.

The old Infirmary was opened on September 1st 1784 and was used as a hospital for the following 183 years, where in its early years of crude surgical procedures, many a patient often suffered horrible mutilations and agonizing death on the operating table. So it comes

The Prospect Centre, Hull.

as no great surprise to learn that over the years this site has been and still is haunted!

But not only haunted by long gone patients, but staff also, for it is reported that during the 1930's a hospital porter took his own life, his body being found in the Porter's lodge and for many years after his lonely spirit was seen wandering the hospital believed to be in search of someone to talk to!

Two years after the new Hull Royal Infirmary opened in Anlaby Road, the old building was demolished and it is recorded that one of the contractors had a ghostly visitor, although what he saw, sadly, was not revealed.

Soon after the land was designated as the site for a new shopping centre. It was said in certain circles that no good would come from using land for private gain especially as it had been given to the people of Hull and their well being over those 183 years.

The new complex opened in the mid-seventies and there have been some strange 'goings on', as eight years ago one newly appointed store manager in the centre discovered, when upon his arrival was told "this place is haunted"!

He soon became aware of the unease cleaners and staff often felt when on the premises after hours.

A catalogue of unexplained events covers such things as the lift indicator moving without an operator, canteen utensils and waste bins strewn around the room, some items being found in unusual places, and feeling uncannily cold to the touch; or the store manager who while working late one night felt most uncomfortable, and came out of his office to notice a hook on a display board "spinning like mad" without cause. That same store has also had items moved around its stockroom again without explanation. Staff from another store are reported to have heard children's voices originating from nowhere.

From the offices within the complex, staff working late have seen mysterious shadowy figures believed to be the same figures that have been seen in the shopping areas and have been described as being in the shape of a nurse or hospital porter in 'whites'.

However, as recently as December 1987, a member of staff in one store was working late when she saw another woman wearing a "very old blue or white dress and a white hat"; wondering who she was she approached her to enquire, only to see her walk behind a column and disappear!

Isn't it strange to think that these ghostly visitors do not seem to appear during daytime and in crowds. However, one may not have been so shy, for on the occasion of one store opening, all the staff posed for a grand opening photo which when processed revealed an unidentified person!!!

Sometime after concluding our researches and writing we received a phone call from our publishers with information regarding a possible 'new' haunting within the Prospect Centre. So wasting no time, the role of researcher was resumed; the outcome of which has revealed the following unexplained mystery.

At the time of writing the following incident has occurred four times on consecutive Saturdays. By request the store identity remains anonymous, but we are allowed to explain what mystified staff have discovered on each of the Saturday mornings.

The cleaners arrived at 7 a.m and were justifiably surprised and annoyed to discover a trail of what appeared to be a distinct path of muddy footprints across the store carpet from the front door past display stands, then disappearing at the oppositie end of the shop with one footprint in partricular halfway through the locked door. It was thought the prints must have been made by a tall person as

46

they were $2\frac{1}{2}$ to 3 feet apart. Adding to the mystery is the fact that the marks on the carpet could not be removed, but faded away unaided around midday. They followed the same route on the first three occasions, but on the fourth, which was overnight on May 6 and 7th 1988, the footprints although again following the same route, started later and ended earlier, but still making the same distinct marks! Strange isn't it?

THE WHITE HANDKERCHIEF

It was 1959 and fifteen year old Angela was an apprentice hairdresser at the Francis Ladies Hairdressers in Jameson Street, Hull, the property long since gone and replaced by the Co-Operative building and British Home Stores.

Angela's experience took place one bright sunny afternoon, when as junior it was her duty, twice a day, to make the tea. This was done on the second floor where such facilities were provided. With the kettle on and waiting for it to boil, Angela used those few minutes to practise plain waving and marcelling on the wig block.

On this occasion her back was to the kettle and window, when quite suddenly Angela's back went "just like ice, absolutely frozen". Somewhat startled, she thought it must be steam from the kettle! But no, how stupid, how could steam make her feel so cold? Nevertheless, she looked over her shoulder expecting to see steam and was astonished to see a man's large white handkerchief suspended by its centre seven inches above her shoulder. It hung there as if held by something invisible. Angela froze in fear, then left the room descending the stairs two at a time, which she recalls as quite a struggle in a tight skirt.

Needless to say Angela didn't return to make the tea that afternoon.

On relating the event, her colleagues laughed as to be expected. However, a senior member of staff told Angela that it must have been "the Old Man knocking about with his bits and pieces!!" Some years later Angela heard from her child's Godfather, a chef at the Skyline Ballroom above the Co-Operative Store, that he knew someone who was afraid to go into the kitchen area which Angela feels sure occupied the same space where she had her experience.... the question remains, who was the old man?

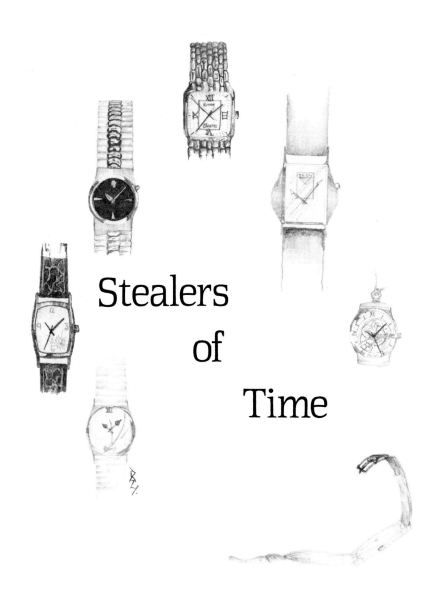

Stealers
of
Time

The Stealers of Time.

THE STEALERS OF TIME

A stone's throw away from Holy Trinity Church in Hull's Old Town, came the mystery of the disappearing wrist watches.

With the lease signed up, the occupiers moved into the property without undue concern, having enquired from the previous tenants if the house was haunted; they had been told "yes, just a bit" and that was all. There wasn't even a second thought in that direction until the night a watch disappeared.

The gentleman had left it on the bedside table, but the following morning it had gone. A search was done, but to no avail; his wife was even blamed for the loss. Thankfully, he had another watch, but the same happened to that, it too disappeared from the bedside table. Now one watch, yes, but two, that's odd to say the least, so he bought a very cheap one: that too went. Puzzled the gentleman acquired more cheap or old watches, and again, in turn they too disappeared; that was until the eighth morning, when his original watch returned, as did each of the others on the following mornings. Apparently this disappearance and return of watches continued for many years and always in a cycle of eight watches. Someone suggested the property be exorcized, but the answer was that as long as it was no more than his watches 'it or they' wanted to play with, then he wasn't bothered; 'it or they' could stay.

SOMETHING SLITHERED IN THE NIGHT

Some stories in both collections have left distinct impressions upon me, to the point of making me very unnerved when writing them, especially late at night. This is not a story as such, but a report of a house with a strange room, or more precisely, a strange bed (and written in the early evening).

The house in Hull's Victoria Avenue has a bedroom that no-one except the brave George would sleep in, but he had been a fighter pilot during the war, so I feel that explains his courage; he occasionally slept in that room just for a laugh, he thought — it was great!!! What happened was that an invisible something 'slithered' over him and he didn't feel it was of human origin! Even his wife walked past that room on the other side of the landing!

PHR

49

THE POLICEMAN

Andrew's father was driving along Hessle Road in Hull, when just near to Neptune Street, Andrew saw a policeman dressed in a very, very old uniform with cape and one of those "great funny hats". He stood on the road in their path. Andrew yelled out "we're going to hit him, we're going to hit him!" His father braked, not having a clue what his son was talking about, but Andrew saw their car pass straight through the policeman!!

A FRIGHTENED DOG

The Vicar had been called to a house in Anlaby Road, Hull, where the residents had seen and heard a ghost moving about upstairs.

Upon arriving at the house and walking down the path, the Vicar was surprised to see a quantity of broken glass strewn along the path. On reaching the front door he noticed the bottom panel of the three glass panels in the door was smashed.

A Frightened Dog.

After introduction, the Vicar remarked upon the broken glass along the path. An explanation followed: apparently the dog had heard the suspected ghost on the floor above and went to "investigate" barking and growling on the way.

What the dog saw is unknown, but something caused the dog to give a loud "yelp" and descend the stairs at such speed it passed clean through the bottom glass panel, and did not return for a couple of hours. When it finally came back it was physically unharmed, but from then on refused to go upstairs!

A NIGHT WITH A FRIEND

For several years, Paul cycled through to see a friend in Anlaby and to save cycling home late after having a few drinks, often stayed the night.

On these occasions he adopted the settee for a bed. One such night, after having been asleep for some hours, he awoke and jumped when he saw an elderly looking man sat in a chair who also appeared to jump, and looking as though he was deep in thought. Once Paul's initial surprise subsided, he assumed the man to be his friend's father, who was probably having a restless night as a result of recently losing his wife, but not wanting to disturb Paul, had quietly entered the room and sat down.

The glow of the street lights illuminating the room was sufficient for Paul to be assured his visitor was who he thought it was, and he soon fell back to sleep.

However, the following morning Paul asked his friend if his father was having restless nights, and went on to relate the previous night's happening.

His friend said he would ask his father if it was him. Paul said not to bother saying anything, but in due course he asked his father outright if he had gone downstairs that night, to which he stated that he had not! Paul's only explanation of what he saw that night was it must have been a ghost, but of whom?

Paul's experiences continue, but this time it's back to September 22nd 1967. He was a student at the old Hull Technical College and travelled to and fro on a motor scooter. On the lunch time of that day, he had the misfortune to be involved in an accident resulting in him sustaining a broken leg, the break being severe enough to

51

A Night with a Friend.

necessitate the fitting of a steel plate, still in place to this day.

Around the same time as Paul's accident, over in Mersey Street, Auntie Peg was experiencing what she believed by now to be a 'visitation' from Paul's late Grandfather (her father), his presence being felt as a "rushing wind" in the hallway. She instinctively knew he was trying to tell her something, this same phenomenon having occurred before. Auntie spoke aloud saying "go away you silly bugger", but the turbulence continued, and by now she was sure there was something wrong within the family.

Auntie Peg began to think there must be something the matter with her mother who lived in Beverley at the time, so she phoned her sister, Paul's mother, who lived nearby. She asked if their mother was well, to which the reply was that she was quite well the last time she had seen her, only a short time ago; Aunt Peg felt relieved, but somewhat curious about "Grandad's visit".

The mystery was solved, when a return phone call from Paul's mum told of his accident earlier!

THE UNCHAINED HEART

It was around 11.30 one night when the vicar received a call from a man sounding rather "flustered". He explained that he and his wife had had a weird experience and they would like some help.

The priest answered their call and upon arrival was told of how the man and his wife had each been sitting by the fireside in their respective armchairs, his wife listening to records while he had dozed off to sleep.

Suddenly a chain had dropped in the wife's lap. Thinking it was her husband who had thrown it, she questioned him in a loud voice which of course woke him. He denied having thrown it at her. How could he? He had been asleep. Naturally she wanted to know where it had come from; her husband suggested it could have fallen from her hair. Her caustic answer told him she didn't carry chains around in her hair and a row developed. Well maybe she had got it onto her hair from a shelf in the room, that was silly as there wasn't a shelf in the room not even a picture rail. The mystery disturbed them so much that it was decided a priest should be called.

The priest enquired from the couple if they recognised the chain. They did, it had been part of a chain and locket. Being in gold with a heart shaped locket, it had been given by Grannie to Greatgranddaughter. Unfortunately the locket had been lost, but the chain had been kept safely just in case the locket should ever be found, its storage being in a little vase on the mantle piece, that useful type of container where pins and buttons get dropped into. The chain had been at the bottom of this vase for many months being buried under other contents. This was the same chain that had suddenly dropped into the wife's lap. The vase was checked and yes, it definitely was that same chain.

The priest was unable to find an explanation, but enquired as to whether Grannie was still alive. No, sadly she had died about a year previous, although this was near to the anniversary of Grannie's passing. Perhaps it was Grannie saying 'remember it's my anniversary, I'm around'. However, the incident was seemingly without meaning. Prayers were said for the peace of Grannie's soul and the house blessed.

The priest was puzzled why it had happened on that day and at that particular time. He asked the wife what she had been doing

The Unchained Heart.

when it happened. Her answer was that she had been listening to a record. The priest asked the title, as she answered her face went white. It was that song made famous by Ray Charles "Take these chains from my heart..." and gasped "'that's weird" she said, realizing what had happened!

As nothing particularly nasty was associated with this incident, the priest left agreeing to return the next day.

The following afternoon he did return to the house to find that there had been a new development in the mystery. Apparently the wife had gone to her mother's in the morning to tell of the previous night's happenings only to be greeted with the news that while spring cleaning she had found the missing heart shaped locket.

We found this a strange story principally due to the uncanny coincidences, firstly the chain dropping into the wife' lap, as she played that record, and on the same day her mother finding in her own house the missing locket. A strange but true story.

HESSLE HAUNTINGS

THE GHOST OF JENNY BROUGH??

Barbara was driving the Land Rover back from Tranby shortly after nine, when suddenly she felt a hand on her shoulder, and knowing there was no one in the back, she was really afraid, but said to "whatever" was responsible "No, no, not when I'm driving" and turned the mirror away so she couldn't see behind her. Foot down, she drove home like a "bat out of hell!"

Still in Hessle and more from Jenny Brough Lane. It was during 1987 at around 3 a.m one night that a family living in that lane were awakened by violent screams of what was thought could be a girl in distress.

The man of the house being concerned at hearing the screams got up, dressed and went out to investigate their origins. He walked both up and down the lane trying to trace the unearthly sounds that penetrated the night, but he was unable to pin point an origin, as at times the air all round shrieked, until it began to fade and ceased completely, his investigations being futile.

Other families of the lane have also heard screams in the night and always investigations have revealed nothing.

It is thought that the screams and other unexplained happenings in the lane are attributed to the ghost of Jenny Brough after whom the lane was named.

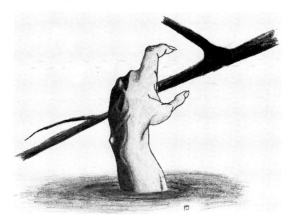

The Ghost of Jenny Brough.

The legend behind the young girl Jenny Brough, according to one school of thought, is that she was murdered, while others say she was accidentally drowned in a pond behind the woods that run adjacent to the lane.

No one really knows how poor Jenny met her untimely death, but if these unexplained happenings can be attributed to her, then she seems to want her presence felt and certainly heard.

The Wildfowler.

THE WILDFOWLER

From the Humber foreshore comes Alec's strange experience. He was a wildfowler; having set off around six that morning, he had been walking along the foreshore for some time when he caught up with an old man also walking in the same direction. For quite a distance they walked and talked about the best places for shooting.

Alec told the old man he thought he would go as far as Crabley. The old man in reply said that he wouldn't, as it was too far for him; these days he just went as far as Little Switzerland. Their conversation continued as they discussed the merits of the various calls wildfowlers use.

Suddenly the old man disappeared. Alec's first thoughts were that he had been consumed in a quicksand or bog; people don't just disappear like that, and so he started a search, but soon realised the ground all around was absolutely firm.

It then struck Alec as to what he had seen — a ghost. He loaded his shotgun and ran away as fast as he could, never daring to return to shoot alone again.

Also from the foreshore comes the tale of the mysterious monks; two girls walking along the foreshore around six one night heard bells and then in the fine mist they saw a group of monks swinging bells. Thinking it was some jokers having a lark, the girls approached them but as they drew nearer, the monks disappeared!!

The Ghostly Monks of Hessle Foreshore.

EAST RIDING HAUNTINGS

A DRIVING FORCE?

The first time it happened was in August 1981. Craig was returning home from the fish and chip shop in Bilton on the B1239 road and had turned off at the 'T' junction that leads to Lelley and crossed the B1240 between Preston and Sproatley. About 100 yards past the crossroads, Craig sensed something come into the car. He turned "completely cold", the hairs on the back of his neck "stood on end" and he lost complete control of the car. He could neither steer nor brake; in fact he admitted to being paralysed with fear, but the car continued on, driving itself for about half a mile. Even when the brakes were applied, nothing happened: It was as though

A Driving Force.

something was keeping his foot off the pedal. Only on reaching the Stag Public House did 'the feeling' leave and Craig regained control again.

Though very shaken by this incident, Craig pushed it to the back of his mind, that is until a night in October 1982 when going to the fish and chip shop in Bilton, it happened again and near the Stag Public House. He recalled the first time his car was taken over, but this time knowing any attempt to control it was futile, he allowed himself and the car to be taken the half mile ride to the crossroads where 'it' left him. Again the return journey was uneventful.

Further research by Craig resulted in the belief that many centuries ago there had been a Priory in the 'affected' area; also the tenants of the Stag Public House at the time in question, told of a sudden chill descending upon them as if someone was there!!

Who or what took control of Craig remains a mystery, but we shall stick to Beverley for our fish and chips!

BRANTINGHAM DALE

By way of an introduction to the next story, we include the following extract from the book "Folklore of East Yorkshire" by John Nicholson and first published in 1890.

"At Skipsea, Cherry Burton, at Leven, at Brantinghamthorpe, and at other places, a headless white lady still affrights the traveller."

The following incident occurred on Thursday September 24th 1987. The four ladies, all members of the Womens' Institute, had been to an 'Old Tyme' musical evening at the Brough WI.

It was just after 10 p.m. when the ladies began their journey by car back to Beverley. They were talking over their evening out, had passed Brantingham church and had entered the dale, when suddenly the car headlights picked out against the blanket of darkness, a very tall figure dressed in white, holding a stick. It stepped onto the road side; not daring to stop, the ladies drove the car past the figure, whereupon already startled they were subjected to "the most terrible piercing screams".

The following day the ladies discussed the night's trauma and contemplated whether the police should be notified, as they feared some foul deed may have taken place. Could it have been a practical joke? Or to add a chilling twist, something supernatural.

For the next few days, the ladies followed news reports with more than a passing interest; thankfully there were no reports of foul deeds, and as to a practical joke, 'our' ladies discovered that other WI members following on that same road shortly after, experienced nothing unusual!

We think the above facts would lead one to believe that the apparition seen that night may have been that same one referred to in John Nicholson's book. Subsequent enquiries revealed that the apparition did not appear to have a face and that the scream was recognised as belonging to a woman.

THE PASSENGER

This story has been passed down to Steve from his Grandfather who told of a very unnerving event his father witnessed whilst a coachman.

It was the 18th Century and William had been a coachman for a considerable number of years, his principal job being that of transporting passengers to and from a large East Riding country house.

The place where his experiences occurred is believed to be on what is now the A165 road, but at the time was little more than a cart track and known by many as Coniston Straight.

The Passenger.

61

On this particular evening dusk had enveloped the countryside quickly. William was on a return journey, the darkness making it difficult to follow the path ahead, forcing him to bring the horses to a steadier pace.

His concentration on the horses and the gloom ahead was broken by a sudden awareness of someone sitting next to him. Nervously he glanced to his left, and there he saw at his side in the previously empty seat, the figure of a person.

The horses reared as the frightened William brought them to a halt. With trepidation he stole another look at his passenger. only to discover to his amazement, but relief, the seat was again empty!!

CHERRY BURTON

Three miles North West of Beverley is the village of Cherry Burton; from here we present the following stories, the first as experienced by Peggy and told in her own words:

"Never be afraid of Ghosts", my mother said. "The dead can't hurt you - it's the living you want to watch". So, when I saw a ghost, I had no fears at all.

My sister and I slept in the back bedroom which opened into the large front 'blue room'. This was the room where my parents slept. We could lie in bed and look through into their room. I was ten years old at this time.

There were two staircases. One came up into our room and the front stairs came up to the landing which led into the front rooms. So, when my sister came up to bed, which was half an hour after me, as she was older, she could come either way. This particular evening, I lay awake waiting for her, when I saw a light coming through from the landing. I watched it grow brighter as if someone with a candle was coming up the front stairs (we had no electricity then). I expected it to be my sister of course. Then the brightness increased and a child with very fair hair and a laughing face came into the room. She paused, put a hand to her mouth as if it was some huge joke and flitted across the room and - I presumed - into the cupboard. "Come out" I said. "I've seen you". While I was still thinking whether or not I should go and see, my sister came up the back stairs to bed. I told her what had happened and she went to look in the cupboard, behind the dressing table, and under the bed.

Cherry Burton.

She told me I must have been dreaming. Nobody believed me, or they said they didn't. My father was inclined to think I had made it up to draw attention to myself. However, I did get back at him some years later, which made him think differently.

My father and I were sitting by the fireside quietly reading. We heard the back door open, then the clump of hob-nailed boots come through the dairy, along the wooden passage past the cellar, through the front hall and then stop at the living room door where we sat. We put down our books to await the knock, or someone to come in. There was just silence. "See who it is" said my father.

How could I tell him that a cold shiver had tickled up my spine? We lit a candle and went to investigate (we had electricity in the living room only at this time). But there was no-one there. We searched the house upstairs and down. We looked in the pantry, the cellar, even the attics, still we found no-one. We always refer to this phenomenon as our "ghost in hob-nailed boots".

Not long ago my cousin came to live in the cottage that adjoins the big house and was at some time a part of it, so we believe. My cousin and his wife said that although they never saw anything strange, quite often the room would become icy cold, the dog would howl and its hair would stand on end.

When they left another family came to live there. An elderly visitor one evening was sitting on the settee by the fire. While her host was in the kitchen, the guest looked up to see a small girl quite happily sitting there too.

The girl disappeared as quickly as she had come. My small girl again I wonder?

The Bay Horse public house in Cherry Burton is also understood to have a ghostly visitor; it is said to be that of an elderly lady dressed in black.

Apparently, the story is thought to originate many years ago when an elderly man, who was very much a regular at the pub, spent most of his time and money on drink. Consequently , his poor long suffering wife always knew where he was, and so it is rumoured that her restless spirit still goes in search of him!!

THE MOTORCYCLIST

It was around 1.30 a.m. and Brian, his wife and two children were returning home from York. Their children were sound asleep in the back of the car.

Entering Market Weighton, on that gentle curve just before the town centre, both Brian and his wife were surprised to see a motorcyclist in black leathers laid spread-eagled on his back, on the opposite side of the road; but if this was an accident, where was his motorcycle?

Immediate concern filled them both. Brian stopped the car with a view to helping, but felt quite uneasy, fearing the possibility of suddenly being "jumped" or attacked by others possibly in hiding.

An approaching car could be heard in the distance; it sounded unusually loud, sufficient to heighten their concern for the man laid there.

Brian's wife realised there was a hand lamp in the glove compartment and thought it may be useful, both thinking they should at least take come preventative action to protect the person laid on the road.

Brian and his wife only turned their eyes away briefly in opening the car doors to get out, but in those seconds, the motorcyclist had disappeared.

Realising there was no longer a body on the road, they both quickly got back into the car, locking the doors fearful of being mugged.

Thankfully nobody appeared, the night again presenting the same deadly silence which had greeted them on arriving in Market Weighton, that is with the exception of that sound of an approaching vehicle, but that too was a mystery for Brian has no recollection of seeing the vehicle he heard approaching!

THE SPIRIT OF WOODHOUSE FARM
HOLME-ON-SPALDING MOOR

I first met David Bowman in the Beverley Public Library; he was researching material for a proposed book, as was I. Our paths crossed, and we entered into a conversation on our respective works.

His research project was similar in nature to one of our earlier publications. I suggested he might find it helpful to look through the draft manuscript. He welcomed the opportunity. The following day David joined us at the Playhouse to do just that. During the course of the morning, the conversation turned to our Ghost Book which led David on to tell us of his own family's encounter with the unknown. A bit of friendly persuasion resulted in the following account of events that have affected the Bowman family for almost three generations. We now present their tale as we received it, in the words of Mrs Bowman and son David.

Mrs Bowman remembers the spring of 1950 as she saw for the first time what was to be her home for the next seven years.

"The farmhouse was typical of its day, four bedrooms, water drawn from a pump outside and no electricity. The only surprise was that the existing owners' son slept in his parents' bedroom even though one of the adjoining bedrooms had been specially decorated for their little boy. Also that particular bedroom had the only wooden floor upstairs consequently it was the warmest bedroom,

The Spirit of Woodhouse Farm, Holme-on-Spalding Moor.

but the door was kept locked which we thought strange. However, we were soon to know why.

Once we moved into the farmhouse, my husband's brother moved in with us to work on the farm prior to his National Service. We gave him the 'little boy's bedroom' as it was the warmest. Each morning when he woke up, he found that the trapdoor in the ceiling to the attic had been lifted off. This trapdoor had to be pushed up and lifted over a ridge. We asked my brother-in-law to stop opening it, he adamantly denied touching it. We then began to realise why the little boy slept in his parents' room!

We moved my brother-in-law into another bedroom and kept his old room locked. Each morning we looked in and always the trapdoor was open. We then started to notice other 'things'. The stairs creaked on certain steps, so when we heard footsteps on the stairs, we would try to catch a glimpse of the 'ghost', but never did see it; also the eyes of our Alsatian dog would follow something as if a person was moving across the room. The door between the passage and the kitchen had a large gap under it and we would often see the shadows of feet moving in the passage, especially when the sun was shining bright; it was so plain to see.

With the arrival of our son David, the whole atmosphere began to change. Our spirit became less active. It was then that we began to believe it was of a woman, who may have died in childbirth or possibly lost children of her own at an early age. Even so, at certain phases of the moon, our dog would start howling and the baby would scream for no apparent reason. It was very unnerving.

After the birth of our second son, Paul, (both were actually born in the farmhouse) a great peace came to the place. The trapdoor very rarely moved after that.

It was with great regret that we had to leave the farm in the spring of 1957. We thought that the spirit might become restless again. But as the people moving in had children, we felt that perhaps it would be alright. We told no-one in that area of our experiences, as they may have thought us unbalanced.

Our son Paul was always drawn to the farm and when home from London, he would drive out there to look at it. The very last time he saw the farmhouse, the windows were boarded up and so he decided to make enquiries. A lady living in a caravan in the farmyard told him that the house was now unsafe and was going to be demolished in the near future. She allowed him to go into his birthplace for one last look round. Paul being curious, headed for what was the 'little boy's bedroom'. The door was locked, but the key was there, and so he went inside. On entering, his eyes were drawn to the trapdoor; wooden battens had been nailed across it so as to securely hold it in place. Obviously 'things' had happened again after we had left the farm.

We would never have secured the trapdoor, feeling that it would have been wrong, better for our spirit to roam free.

The house was pulled down in the late seventies, our eldest son David collecting a number of bricks to keep as a reminder of the farm.

My husband and I have never experienced anything like this since we left the farm."

Although Mr and Mrs Bowman were never troubled by the spirit again, there were to be further strange happenings as told by their eldest son David who now continues the story......

"I have now had three of the farmhouse bricks in my home for about twelve years. Prior to getting the bricks, our house was a normal, newly built semi-detached house in Pocklington.

But things changed immediately I brought the bricks home. The trapdoor to the loft space would be in place when we went to bed and in the morning it was pushed up and slid over into the loft. This happened repeatedly, also my wife and I saw shadows and heard footsteps; several of our relatives and friends experienced these 'happenings' too, but none more so than my dear mother-in-law, Doris.

We went on holiday to Italy and left the keys with Doris so she could keep an eye on the house. One day on entering it, she got the surprise of her life. She saw that all moveable objects had been upended, the birdcage was laid on its side across the floor, plants had been strewn all over, also the ornaments were on their sides. It was as if a strong gust of wind had blown through and tipped everything over. On checking, Doris found all windows and doors were still secure. To this day we do not know how or why it happened. Doris only told us of this sometime after when she heard us talking of our experiences. She thought I would brand her as a crank.

When our daughter Hayley was born in 1979, life calmed down again just as it had at the farm. That is until we moved to our present home. This time I left the bricks in the garage which is attached to the house, thinking it was the best place for them.

Almost immediately we started getting really loud banging on the living room wall. I would chase round to the garage to see what was going on. Needless to say there was nothing to see. The banging stopped several years ago and to date we have had no further bother from our spirit".

Isn't it strange to think that 'the spirit of Woodhouse farm' seems to have remained and travelled within those bricks.

THE VICTORIA HALL POCKLINGTON

A second story from David Bowman tells of what may be the ghost of poor 'Mary' who is reputed to haunt the Victoria Hall in Pocklington.

The following is told in David's own words.

"During the early part of this century, a converted flax mill was used as a Public Hall and named the Victoria Hall where various

Steve Oldfield 1988

The Victoria Hall, Pocklington.

types of functions took place including concerts, banquets, sales, parties and dances.

It was during World War 1 at one of these dances that the story begins. Soldiers billeted in the town used to attend these functions. A couple, Mary, a local girl, and a soldier were seen to leave one particular dance together.

Later that evening the body of the murdered Mary was found in a doorway opposite the Oddfellows Pub. The soldier was traced straight away back to the dance. On being questioned, he stated that it could not possibly be the body of Mary as he had been dancing with her some considerable time after the body was discovered!

The question which has never been answered is how could Mary have been in two places at the same time, dead or alive!

What became of the soldier no-one knows. Of Mary a large number of people are convinced she still visits the old Victoria Hall, or at present the mill belonging to R.M. English & Son Ltd. (though soon to be demolished).

As far as is known no-one has seen Mary, though many of the mill men including myself have felt her presence. Mr Ken Durkin, who works in the mill, recalls a typical 'happening'. "You can be walking around or working away in the mill, when all of a sudden you feel as though there is someone very close to you. On turning around though, there is nothing." Others in the mill have felt a 'cold' presence.

One of the strangest episodes occurred about 5 years ago, when John Hobson and myself were working together on the middle floor of the mill. We both heard quite clearly a voice calling "John, John, John" repeatedly. The voice was not familiar to either of us. We searched thoroughly the middle and upper floors, but found no-one. To this day it remains a mystery, but both John and I know what we heard was very real, yet unreal in another sense.

What will become of Mary when the mill is finally demolished, who knows?!!"

THE PHANTOM AIRMAN

Our friend and typist Anita Wain has allowed us to share the following story, we leave it introduced and told in her own words.

"I don't think I have told you this story before, I can remember thinking that if anyone read it at work they'd laugh at me! But it's funny how many people, some you wouldn't really think of as 'believers' have said how they have enjoyed your first book and how it really makes you think doesn't it?

I don't think so many people would laugh at that story now, in fact others might have 'seen or felt' things as well.

In 1981 I was working in what used to be the old Air Traffic Control Tower when the RAF were at Leconfield.

My office was at the end of the upstairs corridor on the left. One day I walked out of my office and passing the office next door on my left, I noticed a pair of legs from behind the unit in the centre of the room. Normally I wouldn't have given them a second glance, but they were covered in blue RAF trousers, with black boots. Working for the Army and always seeing 'green', it was always nice to see a 'blue job' about the place once in a while.

I carried on into the office I was originally heading for, had my query answered, and headed back to my office.

I instinctively looked back into the office next door to see if the RAF chap was still there. He was; sitting I presumed in the window (the windows upstairs had those very wide window sills, so you could sit in them and look out over the airfield towards Arram, this I presumed he was doing) although I couldn't still see the top half of him because of the unit.

Knowing that the Staff Sergeant who worked in that office was out, I called to the RAF man from the doorway, "Are you waiting for someone, or can I help you?" The legs moved, or rather disappeared.

I glanced around the centre unit and there was no-one there. There was no-one in the room except for me and there was only one door in and out, and he couldn't have got those windows open fast enough to have got onto the roof below!

What do you think, an airman who used to work there years ago?"

A.W.

SUNDERLANDWICK HALL

Sunderlandwick Hall is about two miles south of Driffield and is believed to be haunted, although nothing is recorded as having been seen there. However a house-keeper many years ago told of strange and eerie sounds heard mainly at night of wet feet slapping along the corridors.

The owner of these wet footsteps has never been positively identified, but it is popular local belief that they were associated with the death of a negro servant who was murdered around two hundred years ago!

We were interested to learn that in support of this story a one-time owner of the Hall, Major Frederick Reynard, spent a considerable amount of time in Africa, as did some of his forbears, so it is more than likely that they could have had Negro servants.

THE MYSTERIOUS CYCLIST

It was during the early 50's that Fred recalls his ghostly experience.

He, his friend and their wives were driving home from Bridlington one night. Passing through Brandesburton they turned round a blind bend on the hill overlooking the gravel pit, when suddenly Fred and all three of his passengers saw, what Fred remembers with

*The Mysterious
Cyclist.*

vivid detail, a man dressed in a long overcoat and flat cap on a very
old type of bicycle riding directly in front of them. Fred brought the
car to a 'screeching' halt and fearing the worst the four of them leapt
out of the car to look for the cyclist they had presumably hit and to
render him any help possible. However, there was no trace of an
injured man or a damaged bicycle; furthermore, there was no
damage to the car.

This story cannot be explained as such, but could this possibly
have been the ghost of some unfortunate accident victim of the past
from that nasty bend?

THE HAUNTED TRAWLER

Any haunting is frightening, but just imagine what life must have
been like for the crew of a haunted trawler, and remember at sea
there is nowhere to run to escape.

This is the story of one such trawler, the Bridlington based
"Pickering".

It appears she started her life around the shores of Ireland,
registered under the name "Family Crest", later changed after a
crew member was lost overboard under strange circumstances.

Another contribution to the vessel's unhappy background came

The Haunted Trawler, Bridlington.

73

when a second crew member took his own life (it has been said that the victims of these tragedies were father and son).

The "Family Crest" left Irish waters and, re-registered, found a new home at Bridlington, where the new owners took to the helm oblivious of the vessel's grim background...... but soon the crew became aware of things not being quite as they should be. The radar would without explanation start operating in reverse, and even with the input terminals reversed, it still operated in reverse again! Expert checks were carried out to no avail. The ship's steering often gave cause for concern, faltering frequently, resulting in the "Pickering" going round in circles.

Repeatedly the engines stopped for no reason, lights "switched" themselves on and off, and the normal well heated cabins became inexplicably freezing cold; but even stranger was the mysterious figure with a black cap, seen wandering the decks! The question was asked 'could it have been a crew member?' Apparently not!

Most of these mysterious occurrences were faithfully reported in some national newspapers and on television, but in addition to these reports, we also heard that things moved about on their own accord and impressions were formed in the bunk bedding giving the appearance of someone laying on it!

No logical explanation could be found for any of these "happenings", so the conclusion was arrived at that the "Pickering" must be haunted!!

The question then arose 'could these happenings or hauntings be in some way associated with poor fish catches?' Yes or no, the crew were forced into a position of having to claim benefit, which in turn led to professional help being sought. This came in the welcome person of the Reverend Tom Willis of Bridlington, who after hearing and studying the incidents set about exorcising the vessel. The "Pickering" was taken about a mile out from the harbour; there the Reverend Tom performed the necessary blessings throughout the vessel to put any disturbed spirits to rest. From that day on it appears all unpleasantries ceased.

An interesting footnote to this story comes from early 1987, at the time the original 'Ghost Collection' was under discussion with the Reverend Tom. On one occasion I 'phoned him to be told that only minutes before speaking to me he had a call from the skipper of the "Pickering" to say that they had just landed their best catch to date!

PHR

OUR SECRET HAUNTINGS

The following stories all originate from the East Riding and were told on the condition that not only did we respect the names of those concerned and change them, but also that their geographical position in the area should not be revealed.

The only story not from our area is "The Little Brown Dog"; however the people concerned are, and as we liked it, we decided it could stay.

THE SOLDIER

Set shortly after the First World War, this story tells of the night two sisters had a visitor. They had been awakened by something, but were not sure at first what. Strangely the whole room was illuminated and there in the doorway a soldier from the First World War stood motionless. Both girls were petrified and sought refuge under the bedclothes, neither daring to look at him again. The following morning they told their parents what they had seen, both girls being chastised in disbelief.

The Soldier.

The story now advances many years. One of the sisters stayed at home to look after her mother; it was in the latter years of mother's life that the story continues. One night she awoke and said to her daughter that she would like a drink of water, so the daughter then in her 60's, set off downstairs to fetch one, when suddenly mother called out "No don't go, come back". The daughter asked her mother what was wrong; mother's reply came as quite a surprise for she said "I've just seen what you saw all those years ago, I've just seen a First World War soldier standing in the doorway"; that same doorway!!

THE NIGHTGOWN

Barbara's daughter, Sue, just couldn't resist buying the charming white Victorian nightgown, but her old cat wasn't too keen, and showed it the night it jumped onto Sue's bed. "All of a sudden it went all electric, you know how cats do" and shot off the bed in apparent fear, but it wasn't until after Sue's "visitors" that she recognised the possible reason for the old cat's speedy departure.

The Nightgown.

Barbara worked for the Samaritans and on this particular night was called out, so in answer took the car and left in haste. Before she left, much to her annoyance, the house lights fused. Oh well, her daughter was upstairs in bed, so repairs would just have to wait.

The noise of Barbara's car on the gravel returning around 3 a.m. had awoken Sue. It was then Sue saw her two visitors standing at the side of her bed, the only light in the room emanating from them.

Sue called to her mother who found her very afraid and distressed and went on to tell what had happened minutes earlier. Apparently she had seen very clearly two little girls in cotton dresses with pinafores, but with such sad faces.

At this point Sue was not afraid, though feeling as if she were somehow intruding upon them, they just stood there sadly looking at her as she lay in bed. It was only as they drifted into the fireplace and disappeared that the fear of what she had just seen hit Sue. Her mother had to spend the remainder of the night with her.

For help, Barbara made a call to the Reverend Tom Willis who in turn sent a psychic medium round to the house in an attempt to discover a possible cause or reason for the appearance of the girls.

Questions were asked about whether something had recently been bought. Thinking it was furniture Barbara answered no, to which the investigator went on to say they had bought something and it was white. It suddenly dawned on Barbara and Sue — no it couldn't be, not the nightgown, but it was. That nightgown had belonged to the mother of those two girls, who had died wearing it, with her daughters looking on.

Sue was advised not to wear it anymore and it was suggested that it be destroyed, but Sue said if that nightgown mattered so much to the girls, how could she destroy it? So now wrapped in tissue paper that nightgown remains unworn, still with the memory of that night.

THE VISIT TO THE BATHROOM

The teller of this story had been invited to a dinner party. During the course of the evening, one of the guests enquired of the hostess if she might use the bathroom; another guest also seized the opportunity for a visit. The hostess jumped to her feet saying "I'll show you the way", but strangely she lingered around outside the door; how odd, thought the two users of the facilities. Having found the loo, the return was no problem.... so why the escort back they wondered?

Later that evening the situation was again repeated, the hostess escorting and waiting for the guests outside the bathroom! A puzzled look on a guest's face brought forth an explanation — you see the house had a ghost; he was a man wearing a top hat and frock coat who walked constantly on the landing. The hostess hadn't wanted her guests frightened should they bump into him.

Coincidentally the ghost was the father of one of the guests at the party and she too had seen him at the house. It is understood that the man loved the house very much, but had taken his own life there by hanging and had really never left!!

THE BUTTERFLY

Tragedy hit the family when their young daughter Kim, went into hospital for a relatively minor surgical procedure. Sadly due to unexpected complications, Kim died.

Kim had been a lively outgoing girl with many friends who had valued and respected her, this being established on the day of the funeral; so it was no real surprise that many of her friends turned up to pay their last respects.

Unfortunately, the large number of mourners was far in excess of her mother's expectations, who had wanted a private family funeral.

Mother's distress came through so strong that a brittle atmosphere developed with her husband, that is until the appearance of a Red Admiral butterfly in their home. This had a remarkable calming effect, but how unusual it was to see the butterfly so far out of season. It reminded them of their daughter Kim, and her fascination for butterflies, especially the Red Admiral.

On returning home from the funeral, the butterfly was found dead in a small glass bowl in Kim's old room. A cover was put over the top to preserve its beauty.

Kim's brother had applied for a job abroad and although enthusiastic, had reservations, and doubted his ability in so many ways, especially the qualifying exam and interview.

Whilst walking to his interview, he was still unsure. Suddenly, a Red Admiral butterfly alighted on his sleeve and in his mind he 'heard' a voice urging him to "go for it". He felt sure Kim's encouragement was there.

He was successful.

THE CLAIRVOYANT

Whilst researching a haunting, we came across the following story; only the name has been changed.

Allison was only 10 when her Mum died. Mum was a clairvoyant and as she lay on her death bed, told Allison she would pass on the gift to her. Mum's hand gripped Allison's wrist tightly, so tight that when life had expired, the attendant nurse had to remove the hand from its grip on Allison's wrist, leaving an impression from the thumb on the young skin. That thumb print has remained.

Only when Allison reached the age of 14 did she realise the full clairvoyant potential she had been given.

It was around 9 o'clock one night whilst Allison was playing the piano, when to say the very least, a bizarre thing happened: water began to pour from her finger tips onto the keyboard; Allison feared this was some sort of warning.

Her Father was travelling to France the next day, so when he arrived home later that evening, Allison begged him not to go, for she knew something awful was going to happen.

Dismissing her suggestion as ridiculous he sent her to bed.

Sometime later, Allison answered the door to the Police, who wished to speak to her Father, so he was called.

They brought tragic news. Allison's brother had been drowned in a brickyard pond on a farm just outside Hull. Sadly he had been wearing heavy rubber waders which had afforded him little chance of survival, hampering his attempts to save himself, when his skylarking turned to tragedy.

Allison asked the Policeman if the accident had occurred at about 9 o'clock...   He told her it had!!!

THE LITTLE BROWN DOG

The children had played with the little brown dog for a long time that morning and thoroughly enjoyed themselves. The following day they went back with a request to the owner, could they play with the dog again? The owner somewhat puzzled asked which dog? The children went on to describe the little brown dog they had played with the day before.

Not knowing what to say and avoiding the awful truth, she just said "I don't think you can play with her today".

It had been her little dog, but it had died 3 months earlier!

And so we close our second collection of hauntings. Now ask yourself, do you believe in ghosts? With so many strange and eerie happenings taking place perhaps you should – it could be your turn next.....